Loony Laws & Silly Statutes

SHERYL LINDSELL-ROBERTS

ILLUSTRATED BY MYRON MILLER

Sterling Publishing Co., Inc. New York

To Marc and Eric . . .
my wonderful sons. From when they were little tykes, our house was
filled with wall-to-wall children who turned our Currier and Ives
snowfalls into a yard with footprints and snow mountains and who
turned our basement into a chemistry lab, a stage for puppet and
magic shows, a detective agency, and everything else for which they
could find an inch of space. I knew then that the only way to
survive was to have a sense of humor.

Library of Congress Cataloging-in-Publication Data

Lindsell-Roberts, Sheryl.
    Loony laws & silly statutes / Sheryl Lindsell-Roberts ;
illustrated by Myron Miller.
        p.   cm.
    Includes index.
    ISBN 0-8069-0472-0
    1. Law—United States—Humor. I. Miller, Myron,
1948– . II. Title. III. Title: Loony laws and silly
statutes.
    K184.L56 1994
    349.73′0207–dc20
    [347.300207]   93-42066
                                      CIP

10 9 8 7 6 5 4 3

Published 1994 by Sterling Publishing Company, Inc.
387 Park Avenue South, New York, N.Y. 10016
© 1994 by Sheryl Lindsell-Roberts
Illustrations © 1994 by Myron Miller
Distributed in Canada by Sterling Publishing
℅ Canadian Manda Group, P.O. Box 920, Station U
Toronto, Ontario, Canada M8Z 5P9
Distributed in Great Britain and Europe by Cassell PLC
Villiers House, 41/47 Strand, London WC2N 5JE, England
Distributed in Australia by Capricorn Link (Australia) Pty Ltd.
P.O. Box 6651, Baulkham Hills, Business Centre, NSW 2153, Australia
Manufactured in the United States of America
All rights reserved

Sterling ISBN 0-8069-0472-0

Contents

Before You Begin

Imagine yourself being the only person on this planet. You'd be living in a constant state of accord. (So . . . you'd be a little lonely.) You'd have no one to differ with your opinions, no one to violate your rights, and no one to injure your health or welfare. But add just one person, and what do you have? Conflict. Antagonism. Strife. (Just look at Adam and Eve.) Eventually you'd need rules and regulations or each of you would struggle to serve your own interests. Therefore, laws are necessary to maintain order in a civilized (and, yes, I like to think we are . . .) society. But did you ever wonder how laws started?

The most basic laws are rooted in the early standards imposed by the family patriarch for the benefit of the family. Families eventually banded together to form tribes

5

and tribal law prevailed, giving power to the wisest and/or strongest of the group. Eventually society developed and land ownership became commonplace. The need to recognize the rights of others soon became apparent. Therefore, early laws were designed to protect us and our property and deny us the right to harm others and their property. Thereafter, laws were enacted at specific points in time to respond to specific needs. For example: "No dog shall be in public without its owner on a leash."

Some laws have deep-seated roots and have been modernized over the years. Some are just hanging around, and others are out-and-out bloopers. For example, in Kansas: "When two trains approach each other at a crossing, both shall come to a full stop and neither shall start up again until the other has gone."

The research for this book has spanned many years, and it's difficult to verify that each law still exists. I've, therefore, relied on the many wonderful people who contributed to this book, each of whom is thanked at the end. So, it's quite possible that some of these laws have been repealed in recent years. But they've probably been replaced by new laws that will seem as ridiculous to future generations as these do to us.

1.
And Away
We Go!

What Would Henry Ford Say?

In Tennessee, you cannot drive a car while you are asleep.

In Cleveland, Ohio, you cannot operate any motor vehicle while sitting in someone's lap.

In Macomb, Illinois, it is illegal for an auto to impersonate a wolf.

In New York, blind men are forbidden to drive automobiles.

In Milwaukee, a motorist cannot park an auto for more than two hours unless hitched to a horse.

In California, a woman in a housecoat is forbidden to drive a car—and in Alabama you cannot drive a car while barefoot or in bedroom slippers.

In Minneapolis, anyone who double-parks an auto, shall be put on a chain gang and fed bread and water.

In Rutland, Vermont, your car is forbidden to backfire.

In Glendale, Arizona, a car is forbidden to back up.

In Youngstown, Ohio, it is forbidden to run out of gas.

In Omaha, Nebraska, each driver on a country road is required to send up a skyrocket every 150 yards, wait eight minutes for the road to clear, and then drive cautiously, blowing the horn while shooting off Roman candles.

In Massachusetts, it's illegal to shave your whiskers while you're driving.

In Decatur, Illinois, it is illegal to drive an auto without a steering gear.

In Emporia, Kansas, when an auto approaches the city limits, a passenger from said auto must precede the auto on foot and warn people that it is approaching so that all horses can get out of the street.

In Ohio, driving your auto in any downtown district was deemed illegal.

In San Francisco, you'd better not get caught wiping your car with used underwear. It's unlawful.

In Memphis, Tennessee, a woman cannot drive a car unless a man is running or walking in front of the car waving a red flag to warn approaching pedestrians and motorists.

In Transit

It is illegal in the state of Florida to transport livestock aboard school buses.

Bullfrogs cannot be exported out of Arkansas.

Transporting a stolen hemlock, cedar, or spruce is illegal on a public highway in Vermont.

Moving Right Along

Unless you have permission or it is a true emergency, jumping from a plane or dropping an object from a plane is illegal in Vermont.

An ordinance in Brewton, Alabama, specifically requires all people on city streets to either walk or ride. They cannot crawl, sleep, or stand.

In Johnson City, New York, a person is not allowed to wander from the left side of the sidewalk to the right.

In San Francisco, it is illegal to discard a boat or an ark on any submerged street.

In Youngstown, Ohio, it's illegal to ride on the roof of a taxi.

In Washington, D.C., all taxis must carry brooms and shovels.

In Albuquerque, New Mexico, a cabbie is forbidden to reach out and pull prospective passengers into the cab.

And it's against the law in Maine to walk down the street with your shoelaces untied.

Atlanta, Georgia, forbids "smelly people" to ride public streetcars.

In Spring Valley, N.Y., anyone riding a tricycle on the sidewalk will be subject to a fine.

In Canada, it's illegal to board a plane while it's in flight.

In Marblehead, Mass., it is illegal to cross the street on Sunday, unless it is absolutely necessary.

In Thomasville, North Carolina, airplanes are forbidden to fly over town on Sundays during the hours of 11 a.m. and 1 p.m.

Disorderly Conduct

In Florida, anyone found underneath the sidewalks will be found guilty of disorderly conduct.

You're On The Right Track . . .

The legislature in the state of Kansas passed a law stating: "When two trains approach each other at a crossing, both shall come to a full stop and neither shall start up again until the other has gone."

In Illinois, a conductor *must* wear "his" hat while collecting fares.

In the state of New York a traffic law states: "Two vehicles that are passing each other in opposite directions shall have the right of way."

In Minnesota, you risk going to jail if you are found standing in front of a moving train.

No railroad train may roll through Gainesville, Florida, faster than a man can walk.

It's a crime punishable by death to put salt on a railroad track in Alabama.

Lights Out

In San Diego County, California, the Board of Supervisors recently enacted a statute that requires all commercial lighting in the unincorporated parts of the county to be turned off at 11:00 p.m.

The Reason: The light pollution was affecting the performance and results of the astronomers at the world-famous Mount Palomar telescope!

To show their appreciation, the scientists named an asteroid for San Diego.

2.
Home
Suite Home

Just Kid-ding

In Jupiter Inlet Colony, Florida, stubborn children are considered vagrants.

Thank goodness Ringo, John, George, and Paul were from Liverpool because it's against the law in Mesquite, Texas, for youngsters to have unusual haircuts.

In Indiana, a parent cannot drink beer if a child is in the room.

In the state of Washington, it's illegal to pretend that your parents are rich.

In Lynn, Massachusetts, babies may not be given coffee.

In the state of Washington, it's illegal to sell comics to minors if the comics might incite them to violent or immoral acts.

Kids in Fort Wayne, Indiana, can't sell their parents' jewelry.

Massachusetts passed a law in 1648 deeming that if a man has a stubborn or rebellious son who disobeys his father and/or mother, said son shall be put to death. *(This law has been repealed by the legislature.)*

In Roderfield, West Virginia, only babies are allowed to ride in baby carriages.

If you live in the state of Louisiana, you can grow as tall as you want.

Not at School

It is illegal in Vermont to allow your sheep to run wild in a schoolyard.

The Family That Prays Together . . .

Ministers in Pennsylvania cannot perform a marriage ceremony if the bride or groom is drunk.

In Vermont, you could be fined up to $200 if you denied the existence of God.

In Kentucky, it's illegal to use a reptile during any part of a religious service.

It's against the law in Key West, Florida, to spit on the floor of a church.

The state of Massachusetts forbids the eating of peanuts in church.

Spokane, Washington, had a law making it illegal for a race horse to interrupt a religious meeting.

And racing horses is banned on Good Friday and Easter Sunday in Delaware.

Bah, Humbug!

In 1659, Massachusetts outlawed—of all things—Christmas. The law stated that "anybody found observing Christmas in any way" would be fined five shillings.

A member of the city council introduced a bill in Albuquerque, New Mexico, banning Santa Claus.

House Rules

In California, a housewife can go to jail if she does not cook her dustcloth after using it.

In Jackson, Mississippi, if you want to set fire to your house, you must first remove the top.

In Belhaven, North Carolina, there was an ordinance permitting a sewer service charge of "$2 per month, per stool." That has recently been revised to read "per toilet."

A tenant is forbidden to bite his/her landlord if living in Rumford, Maine.

Don't Touch Me!
You could go to jail in Georgia if you slap an old pal on the back.

Food Junkies

In New Jersey, it is against the law to slurp soup.

It is illegal to shoot open a can of food in Indiana.

The mixing of cornmeal or any other flour with wheat flour is illegal in Maryland.

The maximum degree of insect infestation and mold that may be permitted in cocoa beans is 6%. *(In reality, this is allowed only because it is impossible for anything that is grown to avoid contact with air and earth.)*

In Los Angeles, California, customers in meat markets are forbidden to poke turkeys to see if they are tender.

21

Ostrich steaks are exempt from state sales tax in California.

In Walden, New York, you are forbidden to offer anyone a glass of water unless you have been issued a permit.

In a Pickle

In Trenton, New Jersey, it's illegal to throw a tainted pickle into the street.

In Rhode Island, it's illegal to throw pickle juice on a trolley.

You need a cheesemaker's license to make cheese in Wisconsin. But to make Limburger cheese, you must have a master cheesemaker's license.

A law in Waterloo, Nebraska, prohibited barbers from eating garlic.

In the state of Tennessee, it's illegal to throw a banana peel on the sidewalk.

In Louisiana, it's against the law to steal crawfish.

In Hammond, Indiana, it is illegal to throw watermelon seeds on the sidewalk.

3.
Let's Keep Going

Amusing Yourself

In Gary, Indiana, one cannot attend the theater within four hours of eating garlic.

In Wyoming, it is illegal to obstruct the view of "fellow" spectators by wearing a hat in any public theatre or place of amusement. (You could have to shell out $10 for this offense.)

Wearing a bonnet at a public place of amusement is also not allowed in Montana.

And in Gary, Indiana, a fine could be imposed on any theatre owner who permitted patrons to wear their hats and/or bonnets in the establishment.

Also in Gary a fine of $200 could be imposed upon a child performing as a singer, musician or gymnast. *(This was repealed in 1953.)*

In Ohio, a person exhibiting a puppet show, wire dancing or tumbling could be fined $10 for engaging in "immoral practice."

The Big Apple

In New York, it's against the law to do anything that's against the law.

Is Anybody Inn?

Once upon a time in the sleepy little town of Boston, Massachusetts, a man entered a very posh hotel and requested a room. The desk clerk refused to assign him a room on the grounds that the man was improperly attired for such a classy hotel. Without saying a word the "prospective guest" made his exit. He quickly changed his clothes—donning his best attire, which might have gained him access to Buckingham Palace. He also gathered sheep, cattle and all the livestock he could locate and he and his animals entered the lobby of the hotel. The desk clerk was absolutely aghast! But he had to give the man and all his livestock rooms. Why? There is a law in existence in the Boston area, that any hotel or inn must make rooms available for a man and his livestock.

If you are staying in California, do not peel an orange in your hotel room; it's illegal.

In New Hampshire, it's illegal to register in a hotel under an assumed name.

Have You Ever Heard of the "Nine-Foot Sheet Law"?

In Oklahoma there was a legendary legislator named Alfalfa Bill Murray. He was a rather tall chap and was continually irked when he went into hotels and found the bed linens too short to cover his long, lanky body. So in 1908 he had a law passed requiring all hotels to have nine-foot sheets.

Never on Sunday

"Never on Sunday" is what a Hartford, Connecticut, law says about kissing your wife.

The sale of ice cream was banned on Sundays in Ohio, because it was deemed frivolous and luxurious. Merchants, therefore, began topping the ice cream with scoops of fruit thereby deeming the dish healthy and nutritious. Lo and behold, the "ice cream sundae" was invented.

In Ohio, "sporting, rioting, quarreling, hunting, and shooting" were deemed illegal on Sundays.

Pigging Out

Public eateries in Bristow, Oklahoma, are required to serve each patron a peanut with a shell for every glass of water served.

If you are dining at a restaurant, boarding house, club, or hotel in Wisconsin, the management is required to serve you—*at no charge*—⅔ ounce of their famous cheese, provided you purchase a meal that costs at least 25 cents.

In Marion, Ohio, cream puffs were once declared against the pure food and drug laws.

In Topeka, Kansas, it is prohibited for a waiter to serve wine in a tea cup.

In Vermont, margarine cannot be served in a public eating place unless a notice is displayed that it is being offered.

In Chicago, it is illegal to eat in a place that is on fire.

In Kansas, it is illegal for eateries to serve ice cream on cherry pie.

In Omaha, Nebraska, two people are forbidden to use the same finger bowl.

It is forbidden to eat rattlesnake meat in public in Kansas.

Nebraska tavern owners may not sell beer unless they are simultaneously brewing a kettle of soup.

In Manzanita, Washington, a bartender can be fined for listening in on conversations between patrons.

Xenia, Ohio, has made it illegal to spit in a salad bar.

4.
Boys and Girls Together

The Dating Game

If you are sending a box of candy to your sweetheart in Idaho, it must weigh a minimum of 50 pounds.

In Dyersburg, Tennessee, it is illegal for a girl to telephone a guy asking for a date.

A man could be fined $100 or more in Ohio if he represents himself as unmarried and keeps company with a "female of good character."

Men, in North Carolina: It's illegal to talk to a woman attending an all-women's college while she's on campus.

And women: Never, never propose marriage to a man if you live in or are passing through Whitesville, Delaware. You can be nailed for "disorderly conduct."

In Portland, Maine, tickling a girl under the chin with a feather duster is illegal.

Kissin' Cousins

Kissing on the lips in Riverside, California, is in violation of a local health ordinance, unless both parties first wipe their lips with carbolized rose water.

A kiss in Halethorpe, Maryland, cannot last longer than a second.

Kissing a stranger in Cedar Rapids, Iowa, is illegal.

Any man who constantly kisses "human beings' is forbidden to have a moustache if he lives in Indiana.

Sorry, My Dance Card's Full

In Compton, California, cheek-to-cheek dancing is prohibited.

Nothing shady—but in Monroe, Utah, daylight must be visible between couples on a dance floor.

Wiggling on the dance floor is illegal in Stockton, California.

If a woman is in Bellingham, Washington, she is forbidden to take more than three steps backwards while dancing.

Iowa City and Belt, Montana, have variously banned: the grizzly bear, the bunny hug, the Texas tommy, the turkey trot, the tango, the duck wobble, the angle worm wiggle and the kangaroo glide.

A mayor in Boston once banned midnight dancing within the city limits.

Girls: In Norfolk, Virginia, you'd better not go to a public dance unless you're wearing corsets. That's the law!

The New York State Assembly passed a law outlawing the tango, the rumba, the mambo, and the cha cha.

Infants in Los Angeles cannot dance in public halls.

"Dancing in Public Places" in Minnesota

It's not allowed. Lighting must be very bright.

You must obtain a permit before holding a dance.

No one is permitted to perform any indecent or immoral dances.

Rude or indecent speech isn't allowed, either.

Till Death Do Us Part

If a lady in Dixie, Idaho, berates her husband in public and a crowd gathers, the husband is subject to a fine.

In Kentucky, it is illegal to remarry the same man four times.

In Tennessee, a man is forbidden to divorce his wife unless he leaves her ten pounds of dried beans, five pounds of dried apples, a side of meat and ample yarn to knit herself stockings for a year.

In Delaware, a marriage may be annulled if entered into on a dare.

In Michigan, a man owns his wife's clothes. Therefore, if she leaves him, he can follow her into the street and remove them!

In Lebanon, Tennessee, a husband cannot kick his wife out of bed even if her feet are cold; however, a wife can kick her husband out of bed without provocation.

In West Virginia, first cousins may marry unless the female is 55 years old.

In Virginia, a man can curse and/or abuse his wife provided he does it in a low voice.

In Pennsylvania, a man cannot be accused of desertion if his wife rents his room to a boarder and crowds him out of the house.

Dunlap, West Virginia, has rendered it illegal to tear up a marriage certificate.

In Chillicothe, Missouri, you will be in violation of the law if you throw rice at the bride and groom.

In Colorado, you will be in violation of the law if you throw shoes at the bride and groom.

Just Between Us Girls...

In Los Angeles, California, it's illegal to hang your lingerie in public view.

A Florida law forbids a housewife from breaking more than three dishes a day.

If you're a woman of "notorious bad character," it's illegal to ride a horse through town.

In Oxford, Ohio, you aren't allowed to wear patent leather shoes.

In Gloversville, New York, women wrestlers are forbidden to appear in the city.

If you're a young woman in Corvallis, Oregon, you are forbidden to drink coffee after six in the evening.

In Kentucky: No female shall appear in a bathing suit on any highway unless she is escorted by at least two officers or is armed with a club.

(THE AMENDMENT READS:)

"The provisions of this statute shall not apply to females weighing less than 90 pounds nor exceeding 200 pounds, nor shall it apply to female horses."

"How Old Are You Now . . ."

In Wisconsin: If you are over 21, you are not required to divulge your age. Instead you can use the following code.

A = 20's
B = 30's
C = 40's
D = none of the above

For Men Only

There is a law in Brainerd, Minnesota, requiring every male to grow a beard.

In Illinois, a law requires all healthy males between the ages of 21 and 50 to work in the streets two days per year.

There may be no such thing as a bald man—just one who has grown too tall for his body; however, in New York City men are breaking the law if they enter beauty shops to have their hair regrown.

5.
Beastosaurus Rex

Watch for the Droppings

In California, it is against the law to detain a homing pigeon.

In Utah, birds have the right of way on public highways.

In Vermont, one cannot kill a bird intentionally from an aircraft.

In Oklahoma, it is illegal to rob a bird's nest from a public cemetery.

It is illegal to sell or buy a buzzard, because they are classified as "songbirds," in Ohio.

In Bayonne, New Jersey, it is against the law for a pigeon to fly overhead without a license.

Birds Not Safe in Michigan

Citizens of Michigan may receive two cents for every English sparrow they kill during the months of December, January, and February. (In order to collect, the bird's well-preserved body must be presented to the village or town clerk.)

Crows or starlings are not safe either. Each starling is worth three cents. Each crow is worth ten cents. (You must present at least 50 well-preserved starlings or 10 or more crows.) Killing the wrong bird in any of these cases is a misdemeanor.

Shh . . . Shh . . .

In Berkeley, California, it's unlawful to whistle for an escaped bird before seven in the morning.

In San Antonio, Texas, you can't honk a horn.

In Tryon, North Carolina, it's against the law to play the piccolo between the hours of 11 p.m. and 7:30 a.m.

If Not for Noah . . .

In Atlanta, it is against the law to secure a giraffe to a telephone pole or street lamp.

In Seattle, Washington, it is against the law for goldfish to ride a city bus in a bowl unless they are kept still.

In Los Angeles, it is against the law to have a hippopotamus in one's possession.

In Youngstown, Ohio, it is against the law to keep a bear without a license.

In Missouri, it is against the law to carry a bear down a highway unless it is caged.

In Virginia, it is against the law to drive an unconfined bear down the street.

In Alaska, it is against the law to disturb a grizzly bear for the purpose of taking its picture.

In Galveston, Texas, it is against the law for camels to wander the streets unattended.

In Newton, Kansas, it is against the law to drive buffalo through the streets.

In Arkansas, it is illegal to blindfold cows on public highways.

In Norfolk, Virginia, it is against the law for hens to lay eggs before 8 AM or after 4 PM.

It is illegal in Arizona to shoot or hunt camels.

Be kind to your oysters in Baltimore, Maryland. It is forbidden to mistreat them.

In Washington, D.C., it is illegal to punch a bull in the nose.

In Texas, it's against the law to milk anybody else's cow.

In Baltimore, Maryland, it's illegal to sell live fowl if they are tied by the legs. The crime carries a fine of $2 per bird.

Any animal that is out after dark in Berea, Ohio, must display a tail light.

It's illegal in North Carolina to take a deer swimming in water above its knees.

In Miami, it is against the law to molest an alligator.

In Kansas, it's illegal for chicken thieves to work during daylight hours.

It's taboo to walk your pet alligator down Main Street in Charleston, South Carolina.

If your billy goat is running loose in Wisconsin, you'd better be prepared to pay $5 to the person who finds it.

In Vermont, you can be fined if your swine runs in a public park without the permission of a selectman.

You cannot march your goose down the main street if you are in McDonald, Ohio.

Poor Old Chicken

Do you remember the old joke "Why did the chicken cross the road?"? Answer: *To get to the other side.* Well, in Quitman, Georgia, it's illegal for a chicken to cross the road.

Reel Estate

In Muncie, Indiana, it is forbidden to carry fishing tackle into a cemetery.

In Ohio, fishing with explosives is against the law.

In the District of Columbia, it is illegal to fish on horseback.

In Kansas, you cannot fish with your bare hands.

On the Chicago breakwater, it is illegal to fish in pajamas.

Fish cannot be transported into New York State via parcel post.

Goldfish cannot be used as bait.

Frogs may be taken from their ponds in New York from June 16 to September 30 provided it is between sunrise and sunset.

Any overt physical action intended to frighten fish is prohibited in New York State.

Anyone younger than 16 or older than 70 can fish without a license.

In Illinois, dynamite cannot be used to catch fish.

In Oklahoma, it's a criminal offense to give liquor to a fish.

Never shoot a fish with a bow and arrow in Louisville, Kentucky.

And don't shoot pickerel or northern pike with a gun in Vermont's Lake Champlain.

In the state of Washington, you can't catch a fish by throwing a rock at it.

Also in the state of Washington, you are in violation of the law if you molest a food fish.

In Malibu, California, there is a "Human-Dolphin Shared Environment" law that was enacted to improve the relationship between humans and "local resident" marine life.

Until recently it was illegal to fish for whales off the coast of Oklahoma.

Hee-Haw!

In Lang, Kansas, it is against the law to drive down Main Street on a mule during the month of August unless your mule is wearing a straw hat.

In Baltimore, it is necessary to document any services performed by a jackass.

In Ohio, it is against the law to set a fire under your mule if it balks.

In Arkansas, if your two-year-old mule runs wild and is not claimed within two days, anyone may castrate the animal. (Once this action has been performed, it will cost you three dollars service charge.)

A Hare-Raising Experience

In New York City, one is forbidden to shoot rabbits from the back end of a Third Avenue streetcar when it is in motion.

In Kansas, one is forbidden to shoot rabbits from a motorboat.

In Statesville, North Carolina, it is against the law to race rabbits in the streets.

In Tuscumbia, Alabama, it is illegal for more than eight rabbits to reside on the same block.

6.
Crazy Critters

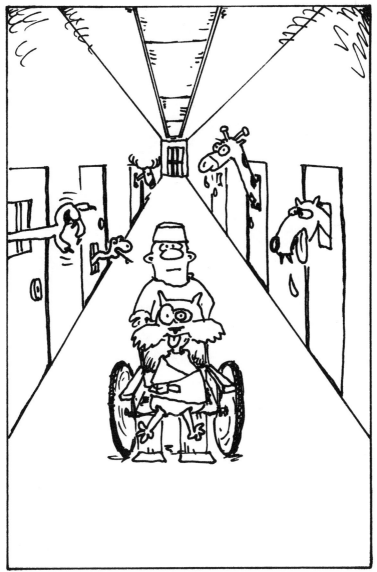

It's a Dog's Life

In Chicago, it is against the law to take a French poodle to the opera.

In Idaho, it is against the law for people to participate in dog fights.

In Massachusetts, all dogs must have their hind legs tied during the month of April.

In Hartford, Connecticut, your dog *cannot* get an education.

In Pauling, Ohio, a police officer may bite a dog in an attempt to quiet him.

In Denver, it is against the law for a dog to transfer on the tramways and all dogs must pay full fare.

In Belvedere, California, an ordinance states: "No dog shall be in a public place without its master on a leash."

Dogcatchers in Houston, Texas, must submit to psychoanalysis to determine their eligibility to chase stray mutts.

In 1936, Denver passed a law stating that a dogcatcher must notify dogs of impounding by posting a notice for three consecutive days on a tree in the city park and along a public road running through the park.

There's a law in Chicago that forbids anyone from feeding whiskey to dogs.

In Joliet, Illinois, if a bitch is found running about, the owner is liable for a fine of $1 to $10.

The Tower of Babble

Speaking English in the state of Illinois is illegal. In 1919, author H.L. Mencken had a statute revised establishing "American" as the official language.

Fighting like Cats
and Dogs

In Barber, North Carolina, it is illegal for cats and dogs to fight.

In International Falls, Minnesota, cats are forbidden to chase dogs up telephone poles. (That also refers to pole cats.)

In Sterling, Colorado, a pet cat cannot run loose without a tail light.

Horsin' Around

In Wilbur, Washington, it is against the law to ride down the street on an ugly horse.

In Fort Lauderdale, Florida, all horses must be equipped with horns and headlights.

In Marshalltown, Iowa, it is against the law for a horse to eat a fire hydrant.

In Fountain Inn, South Carolina, all horses are required to wear pants in public.

If you live in Omaha, Nebraska, you are required to place a hitching post in the front of your house.

In Virginia, it is illegal to permit an unhaltered horse— age one year or older—to appear in any public place of worship.

Horses cannot be turned loose in a burial ground in Vermont.

In Norfolk, Virginia, a horse may not be ridden in the waters of Chesapeake Bay.

Vermont doesn't approve of painted ponies. If you're found painting yours, you will be arrested.

Anyone leaving horses or mules unattended (unless tied to a hitching post) will be subject to a fine in Spring Valley, New York.

In New York City, you can go to jail if you open your umbrella in the presence of a horse.

In Vermont you cannot sell horse urine unless you're licensed.

Changing the teeth of a horse to deceive another individual is illegal in Arkansas.

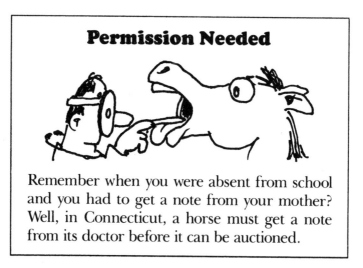

Permission Needed

Remember when you were absent from school and you had to get a note from your mother? Well, in Connecticut, a horse must get a note from its doctor before it can be auctioned.

7.
All in a Day's Work

Splish Splash . . .

A Florida law requires one to wear clothing when taking a bath.

In Carmel, California, a woman cannot take a bath in a business office.

A law in Boston, Massachusetts, has rendered it against the law to bathe without a written prescription from a doctor.

Falling asleep in a bathtub in Detroit, Michigan, is illegal.

Everyone must take a bath on Saturday night in Barre, Vermont.

Having a bathtub in your house in the state of Virginia is forbidden. It must be kept in the yard.

If you live in Minneapolis, Minnesota, and plan to install a bathtub, be certain that it has legs.

In Berkeley, California, residents are required to simultaneously fill bathtubs and unplug them. *This was to drown rats in the sewer system.)*

Taking a bath during the winter months is against the law in Indiana.

Those in the state of Virginia who own bathtubs must pay $30 levy for each.

In Brooklyn, New York, it is illegal for a donkey to sleep in a bathtub.

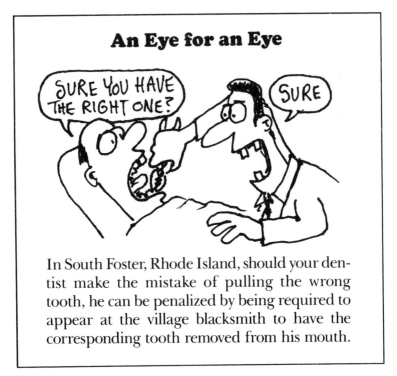

An Eye for an Eye

In South Foster, Rhode Island, should your dentist make the mistake of pulling the wrong tooth, he can be penalized by being required to appear at the village blacksmith to have the corresponding tooth removed from his mouth.

Dress Code

If you are in Nevada, you'd better not have a hatpin stick out beyond your hat more than a half-inch.

In Zion, Illinois, street vendors are required to wear shirts, blouses and shoes.

If you plan to go swimming in Rochester, Michigan, you must first have your bathing suit inspected by the police.

In Elko, Nevada, everyone walking on the street is required to wear a mask.

In Atlanta, it is illegal to dress a mannequin unless the shades are pulled down during the robing and disrobing period.

In Nogales, Arizona, they "let it all hang out." It is illegal to wear suspenders.

A 200-pound woman in Gurnee, Illinois, may not ride a horse in shorts.

Getting to Work

In Altoona, Pennsylvania, it is illegal for a babysitter to clean out the employer's refrigerator.

In St. Louis, Missouri, it is illegal for the milkman to run while making deliveries.

In Indiana, roller skating instructors are forbidden to lead their students "astray" during lessons.

In Wyoming, it is illegal to eliminate cuspidors for the use of employees.

Even if your boss is a stinker, in Michigan it is against the law to put a skunk in his desk.

Uncle Ben's Barber Shoppe

In Erie, Pennsylvania, no one can fall asleep in a barber shop while having his hair cut.

In Alabama, no one can sleep in a barber shop all night.

In Baton Rouge, Louisiana, the state house of representatives passed a law stating that a maximum of 25 cents can be charged to cut the hair of bald men.

In Omaha, Nebraska, it is illegal to shave a man's chest.

In Elkhart, Indiana, a barber cannot threaten to cut off the ears of kids.

In Waterloo, Nebraska, barbers are forbidden to eat onions between the hours of 7 AM and 7 PM.

In Lindenhurst, New York, a woman is not allowed to give a man a permanent wave.

In Milwaukee, barbers cannot use powder puffs to practice their trade.

Shop Till You Drop

It's illegal to sell suntan oil after noon on Sunday in Provincetown, Mass.

If you happen to be on a shopping spree in Joliet, Illinois—beware. It's illegal for you to try on more than six dresses in any one store.

It's also illegal to mispronounce the name "Joliet."

In Owensboro, Kentucky, you may not buy a hat unless your husband has first had the opportunity to try it on.

There's a law in Magnolia, Arkansas, that regulates the sale of green meat.

Can't a Person Get Any Sleep Around Here?

There is a law in Dunn, North Carolina, outlawing snoring and disturbing one's neighbors. The police can impose a 2- or 3-day jail sentence.

You may not sleep in a refrigerator if you are in Pittsburgh, Pennsylvania.

It's illegal in Florida to doze off under a hair dryer.

8.
S.O.S.

That's Killing Me!

If you live and/or work in Natoma, Kansas, it is in violation of the law to throw a knife at anyone wearing a striped suit.

In Frankfort, Kentucky, one is forbidden to shoot off a policeman's tie.

In North Dakota, if a man accused of a felony refuses to accompany you to the police station, you are legally entitled to shoot him.

In Norfolk County, Virginia, you are legally permitted to hunt with a rifle provided you are at least 50 feet off the ground.

South Carolina considers it a capital offense to inadvertently kill someone while attempting suicide.

Anyone in Montana who slays or disables another in a duel must support the victim's family.

Rats!

Kill any of the following in Michigan and you receive ten cents:

Black Rats	Brown Rats	Grey Rats
Norway Rats	House Rats	Barn Rats
	and	
	Wharf Rats	

(In order to collect, their well-preserved heads must be given to the village or town clerk and you must deliver not fewer than five at a time.)

It's a Beautiful World

If you're ugly or grotesque and live in San Francisco, you'd better stay off the streets during certain times of the day.

Go Directly to Jail and Don't Collect $200

In Charleston, South Carolina, a prisoner can be charged $1.00 for the ride to jail.

In White Cloud, Kansas, it is against the law to break out of jail.

In Kulpmont, Pennsylvania, it is against the law to keep a prisoner incarcerated on Sundays.

The state of Illinois permits the imprisonment of animals.

No Ifs, Ands or Butts

No person is allowed to chew tobacco without an M.D.'s permission in Connecticut.

It is illegal to smoke a pipe after sunset in Newport, Rhode Island.

It is illegal to smoke while fishing in Berkeley, California.

What a Dead Beat!

In New York, it is a misdemeanor to arrest a dead man for being in debt.

Funeral directors in Nevada can be arrested for using profane or obscene language in the presence of a dead person.

Until as recently as 1975 it was illegal for a police officer in Maine to arrest a dead body.

Rogues & Vagabonds

In Maryland, persons can be deemed rogues or vagabonds and sent to jail if:
1. they are carrying a picklock, key, jack, bit, or crow in a dwelling house, storehouse, stable, motor vehicle or outhouse.
2. they are carrying a pistol, hanger, cutlass, or bludgeon.

Persons who are not insane are guilty of a misdemeanor in Maryland if they wander about the state and lodge in a marketplace, barn, barrack, outhouse or the open air.

It's an Act of Treason

It is considered treason to wage war against Indiana while living there.

Fire! Fire!

"Practice may make perfect," and in Fort Madison, Iowa, there is a law requiring firemen to practice for 15 minutes before attending a fire.

In Rochester, New York, firemen must wear ties while on duty.

In Zeigler, Illinois, only the first four firemen who show up at a fire will receive financial remuneration for their services.

9.
Fun and Games

When School's Out

In the District of Columbia, it is illegal to fly a kite.

No person over the age of ten may wear and use metal skates in the capitol building in Arkansas.

Sled coasting on highways in Vermont is illegal if it is considered dangerous to any travelers.

Did you ever wonder why Muskogee, Oklahoma, has no major league baseball team? Perhaps it is because there is an ordinance forbidding any member of a ball team to hit a ball over the fence or out of the park.

In Wenatchee, Washington, it's against the law to play baseball in a public place. The law also extends to throwing apples to and fro in alleys. That too is illegal.

If you play hopscotch on the sidewalk in Missouri on Sunday, you will be in violation of the law.

Gone Hunting

In Florida, you are forbidden to hunt or kill deer while swimming.

In Tennessee, you are forbidden to shoot game other than whales from a moving car.

In Fort Hauchuca, Arizona, you are forbidden to hunt buffalo on the parade ground.

In Ouray, Colorado, you are forbidden to hunt elk on Main Street.

In Los Angeles, California, you are forbidden to hunt moths under a street light.

In Cleveland, Ohio, you are forbidden to catch mice without a hunting license.

You cannot pursue wildlife "in or on a motor vehicle or by use of its lights" nor can you "take wildlife from a public highway."

You cannot catch migratory game birds from a motor vehicle or aircraft.

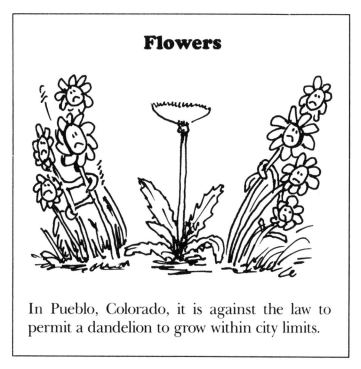

Flowers

In Pueblo, Colorado, it is against the law to permit a dandelion to grow within city limits.

Screwy Law Contest

A number of years ago the Connecticut Department of Consumer Protection sponsored a "There Ought to Be a Law" contest. Here are some of the screwy laws that people found:

In addition to smoking and non-smoking sections, restaurants must have nose-blowing and non–nose blowing sections.

It's illegal to sell boxes of cereal or bags of potato chips unless they are full.

It's against the law to serve soda that has no fizz.

All hamsters must come with a guarantee.

"Have a nice day!"—Now what could be wrong with that? It's illegal to use those words if you're delivering bad news.

If you're going to bare it all on a nude beach, you'd better weigh less than 125 pounds.

If you leave your manure on a public highway, it will automatically become public property.

These Two Laws Should Become Universal

Every law should be written in plain language and should be 50 words or less.

Patients who are kept waiting in a doctor's waiting room may charge the doctor for their time.

No Sneezing, Laughing, or Any Such Thing

It is against the law in Louisiana to gargle in public.

The National Association of Broadcasters forbids any scenes in which someone is gargling.

It is against the law to expectorate against the wind in Sault Ste. Marie, Michigan.

In Waterville, Maine, it's illegal to blow your nose in public.

In the state of Nebraska, it's forbidden to sneeze in public. And in Omaha, it's illegal to burp or sneeze in church.

San Francisco has outlawed the purchase and sale of kerchoo powders and stink balls.

Slippery When Wet

A local ordinance in Brewton, Alabama, forbids the use of motorboats on city streets.

In South Carolina, it is against the law to crawl around the public sewer system without a written permit from the proper authorities.

In the state of Vermont, it is illegal to whistle underwater.

In Lake Charles, Louisiana, there is a law making it illegal for a rain puddle to remain on your front lawn for more than 12 hours.

Durango, Colorado, forbids daytime swimming in either a pool or river.

Bathing in the state of nudity in the waters within the corporate limits of this Village" is forbidden between the hours of 5 a.m. and 8:30 p.m. in Spring Valley, N.Y.

10.
Order
in the Court

Tell It to the Judge

In Los Angeles, if you're weeping on the witness stand in a courtroom, you can be found guilty of misconduct.

In Indianapolis, Indiana, a lawyer asked a criminal court judge for permission to call in a psychiatrist to examine a jury member in a robbery case. The request was denied because there is no statutory requirement that a juror be sane.

Legal Eagles

A law in Maine calls for a legal hunting season on attorneys.

In 1981, Georgia officials were poring through the statutes and they discovered a law that allowed pensions to Confederate widows. During that week, the last widow died and they repealed the law.

In 1985, a legislator in Arizona proposed a law that each candidate have to take an IQ test and the results be posted on the ballot.

Bridgeport, Connecticut, passed a law stating that a city cannot go into bankruptcy. Then a legislator attempted to pass a law that would dissolve the city and divide it into its contiguous suburbs.

A Minnesota tax form asked for all sorts of information. It requested that you fill in your date of birth and your date of death.

Each year the mayor of Danville, Kentucky, is obligated to appoint three intelligent housekeepers to the Board of Tax Supervisors.

Rushville, Illinois, requires a quorum at its city council meetings. If there isn't a quorum, the police are authorized to go out and arrest members of the council and drag them to meetings.

Coming Up Short . . .

A legislator in Maryland who was sensitive about his small stature had the playing of singer-songwriter Randy Newman's song "Short People" outlawed on public radio.

And speaking of short . . . a legislator in Arkansas proposed that the state provide growth hormones to dwarfs.

Banned!

The following books have been banned at one time or another:

Merriam-Webster Collegiate Dictionary (for obscene words) . . . in Carlsbad, New Mexico

The Exorcist . . . in Aurora, Colorado

Slaughterhouse-Five (is now on library bookshelves, but notices will be sent to the parents of any child borrowing the book) . . . in Island Trees, New York

The Stepford Wives . . . in Warsaw, Indiana

Dog Day Afternoon . . . in Vergennes, Vermont

One Flew Over the Cuckoo's Nest . . . in St. Anthony, Idaho

Catch-22 . . . in Strongsville, Ohio

Down These Mean Streets . . . in Queens, New York

Playboy and *Penthouse* magazines . . . in Clay County, Mississippi

Ms. magazine (was ordered removed from high school libraries, but was saved by a court order) . . . in Contra Costa County, California

If Shakespeare Could See This . . .

Hamlet: Sexual references were removed . . . by many publishers.

Macbeth: References to drinking and lechery were removed . . . by many publishers.

Romeo and Juliet: 400 words of "sexually explicit material" were eliminated . . . in the state of New Mexico.

Politics as Usual

In Kansas, an old law prohibits politicians from handing out cigars on Election Day.

In Ohio, if you interrupt a speaker on Decoration Day, you are subject to a $25 fine. (Publicly playing croquet or pitching horseshoes within one mile of the speaker's stand is considered an interruption.)

Corruption at Its Finest

There's an old law in Virginia that is: "An Act to Prevent Corrupt Practices of Bribery by Any Person Other Than a Candidate."

So Sue Me!

You cannot sue the federal government unless you get the government's permission. There are also several states you cannot sue without their permission. (This dates back to the days of sovereignty, when one couldn't sue the sovereign or any of his agents.)

In the state of Oregon, it is illegal to require a dead person to serve on a jury.

Can children sue their mother for damage suffered as a result of negligence during the time she was pregnant with them? Yes, if the child resides in Illinois.

In Vermont, you can collect damages if another person cuts down your tree or defaces your logs.

On the Foreign Front . . .

In Sweden, it's illegal to train your seal to balance a ball on its nose.

In what was East Germany, there was an anti-spy law forbidding you to wave good-bye to somebody from a train window. It could be construed as a code.

This is not a duck law, but in Iceland anybody can practice medicine, providing he/she hangs out a sign that reads *Scottulaejnir*, which means "Quack Doctor."

In Cambodia, there was a time when it was illegal to insult a rice plant.

In the Balanta tribe of Africa, a law states that a bride must remain married until her wedding gown has worn out. If she's desperate to get it over with quickly, she must wait at least one month and then rip up her wedding dress.

In France, a woman was granted a divorce after she told the judge that her husband played the bagpipes and made her keep time with a fly swatter.

In Greece, if a man is caught kissing a woman in public—even if the woman is his wife—he can get the death penalty!

E.T., Phone Home

In the 1950's it was illegal for a flying saucer to land in the vineyards of France. It's now okay.

Be It Remembered:

I gratefully acknowledge the enthusiasm of the following people and organizations whose contributions added great depth and humor to this book.

Stanley Alpert
New City, New York

American Wind Energy
Association
Alexandria, Virginia

Barbara J. Ashworth,
Research Analyst
Legislative Council
State of Rhode Island

Jim Armstrong, Mayor
Torrance, California

Martha G. Barlow, County
Clerk and Treasurer
Hawthorne, Nevada

Mike Brown, Editor,
The Mayor
Published by U.S. Conference
of Mayors

Bureau of Legislative
Research
Little Rock, Arkansas

Robert L. Cable
Legislative Reference Bureau
Harrisburg, Pennsylvania

Anthony J. Celebrezze, Jr.
Attorney General
State of Ohio

City Clerk
Cheyenne, Wyoming

David W. Conover
National Rifle Association of
America

Frank W. Daykin, Esq.
Legislative Council
Carson City, Nevada

Brenda C. Desmond, Esq.
Staff Attorney
Montana Legislative Council

Paul Gellies
Office of the Secretary of
State
State of Vermont

Gorrin, Whitken & Crowley,
Esqs.
Livingston, New Jersey

Linda K. Haberman
Deputy City Clerk
Annapolis, Maryland

Paula Henstridge
U.S. Department of
Agriculture

Robert N. Howell
Executive Director
Georgia Egg Commission

Hubert H. Humphrey, III
Attorney General
State of Minnesota

Wendell C.M. Lee, Esq.
Wine Institute
San Francisco, California

Legislative Council
Helena, Montana

Legislative Council
Providence, Rhode Island

Legislative Service Bureau
Lansing, Michigan

Lothian Lynas
Head Research Librarian
New York Botanical Garden

Abit Massey
Georgia Poultry Federation,
Inc.

Joe Meyer
Wyoming State Legislature

Diane C. McKeown
Account Supervisor
Dudley-Anderson-Yutzy
Public Relations
Incorporated

Irene F. Morrows
Executive Secretary
Nevada Gaming Commission

National Space Institute
Washington, DC

Michael T. Norton, Esq.
Assistant City Attorney
Minneapolis, Minnesota

Mineral County Clerk &
Treasurer
Hawthorne, Nevada

Van O'Steen, Esq.
Phoenix, Arizona

Priscilla Triolo Osterkorn,
Esq.
State of New Jersey

E. Phillips
Library Division,
Department of Legislative
Reference
General Assembly of
Maryland

Kenneth E. Roschke, Jr.
Assistant Attorney General
State of Minnesota

Rockland Audubon Society,
Inc.
New York, New York

Joel Rosenthal, Mayor
Spring Valley, New York

Marsha W. Silver
Assistant Public Information
Director
State of South Carolina

W.R. Souigny
Training Officer, Gaming
Control Board
Carson City, Nevada

Florence Wetzel
Executive Assistant
National Coalition Against
Censorship

About the Author

Sheryl Lindsell-Roberts developed her interest in law when she worked as a legal secretary after graduating from high school. Following the birth of her two sons, Marc and Eric, Sheryl leaped out of the frying pan in the kitchen and into the fires of academia. Several years later, Sheryl received her master's degree in business. Thereafter she co-authored a legal secretary's handbook sold by a major publisher, and developed a paralegal program that she taught at a well-established business school. Sheryl has also written several reference books that have been sold by some of the nation's leading publishers. She's been actively involved in marketing communications and in video productions. One video production was aired on cable television and nominated for an award at the 1992 New England Video & Film Festival.

Sheryl firmly believes that her biggest asset is her sense of humor and that you can survive almost anything in which you can find amusement (even the legal system). Sheryl and her husband, Jon, live in Marlborough, Massachusetts, where they've recently built their dream home. When she isn't writing, Sheryl can be found illuminating the inner reaches of her spirit by travelling, photographing nature, skiing, or sailing *Worth th' Wait.*

Index

95